# Testimonials

# Mercy

"Mercy has such a Christianese reverberation to it, but when I consider it more deeply, receiving it gives me relief and giving it reflects the glory of God. God's supreme mercy requires me to simply accept this most generous gift and then to show gratitude by showing mercy toward others."
**Shelli Wenschlag**, Motivational Speaker
www.immersionministries.org

# Purpose

"Purpose finds you when you pursue the heart of God. It's not a destination but the journey that unfolds as you daily seek God. By seizing opportunities, using gifts and capitalizing on relationships, purpose blooms like a rose bud. Petal by petal, in the right sequence and timing."
**Elaine Q. Potts**, Blogger
www.chooseonething.com

# Grace

"I wore the Christian outfit but underneath I hid all of my brokenness. When I came to Jesus and let His light shine into the dark secrets and shame of my past, I began to experience His *unforced rhythms of grace*." Matthew 11:28-30 (The Message)
**Michelle Viscuse,** Blogger
www.journeypink.com

# Mercy

"The Cross is evidence of God's mercy; that He who knew no sin died in my place. He freely offered mercy when I did not deserve it. God's mercy towards me is truly amazing!"
**Tope Keku**, Speaker, Writer, Bible Teacher
www.hiddentreasuresandriches.com

# Purpose

"Sometimes clear purpose doesn't emerge until after we've been through the refiner's fire. Before I experienced flashbacks from childhood trauma, I felt God's call to be a Christian communicator. After healing, I know God calls me to teach women to live like the priceless treasures God made them to be."
**Lyneta Smith**, Blogger, *Waiting for Applause*
www.lynetasmith.com.

# Grace

"*You just don't know how much I love you*. The last words my father whispered before he slipped into a coma. His last words were to me. God knows what we need even before we ask."
**Sheryl Buckner**, Blogger, Speaker and Author-to-Be
www.SherylBuckner.com

## Books by Melissa Kirk

### Nonfiction

Grace Warrior Devotional Series

Grace Warrior – *Bathed in Mercy, Clothed in Grace*

Grace Warrior – *At the King's Command*

ADVENT– *Celebrate the Coming*

*...watch for more in the Grace Warrior Devotional Series*

# Grace Warrior Devotional Series

*The Grace Warrior Devotional Series* is designed to enhance the reader's relationship with God. Each book in the series stands alone. As a whole, the books in the series build a foundation for kingdom living.

*Grace Warrior – Bathed in Mercy, Clothed in Grace* encourages the reader to focus on scriptural empowerment. This book is especially useful for recalling God's purpose and plan when seeking direction.

It begins with a short introduction. From there, it focuses on the topics: Mercy, God's Plan, My Purpose, and Grace. There are seven sections per subject. Worship reading is first and opens a conversation with God about the topic. The next six readings look at the theme from the perspectives of *Foundation, Acceptance, Belief, Planning, Growing, and Sharing.*

Each reading is short to encourage time for personal interaction with God through his word and prayer. Although numbered for a four-week journey, the reader should dwell on each topic as long as they wish. There is a discussion guide included for those who would like to read and discuss the devotional together.

# GRACE WARRIOR

## *Bathed in Mercy, Clothed in Grace*

Grace Warrior Devotional Series


Melissa Kirk

Grace Warrior

GRACE WARRIOR – *Bathed in Mercy, Clothed in Grace*

Published by Charlene Publishing

Cover Design by oberkromdesign.prosite.com



ISBN-13: 978-0996923118 (Charlene Publishing)
ISBN-10: 099692311X



Published in the United States

First Edition.

To Delinda,

my sweet sister.

♥

Your bubbly personality gives me great joy!

I love you.

# GRACE WARRIOR

## *Bathed in Mercy, Clothed in Grace*

### Contents



### Excerpts

## GRACE WARRIOR

Her position is reflected on the cover of this book.

There was a time when life dumped on, stepped on, and overlooked the woman on the cover of this book. She searched for love, only to find rejection. Lies stripped away her dignity while antidotes for stress left her numb. She did all she could, but it was never enough.

Desperate, she fell to her knees and cried out, "Help me!"

God answered. She's the King's daughter now. She is Grace Warrior, and she's been *bathed in mercy – clothed in grace.*

You can see her next position on the cover of

Grace Warrior –*At the King's Command*

Grace Warrior

Definition:

A child of God, who handles Kingdom business with dignity and determination.

"For God is working in you, giving you the desire and the power to do what pleases him."

*Philippians 2:13*

# Grace Warrior

If you are my sibling-in-Christ, then I know you've experienced the mercy of God. He met you at the cross. He stripped off the dirty, ugly, often tattered and worn-out life clothes, and as Psalm 103 says, he removed those rags as far as the east is from the west. At that moment, you became clean. And vulnerable.

I don't do clean well. By the end of the day, I will have evidence of everything I've eaten and a lot of what I've said, all over me.

Vulnerable? When I find myself in unknown territory, I suddenly feel inadequate.

Mercy removed our guilt, but clean and vulnerable sounds hard, doesn't it? Well, we can thank God that he didn't stop with just mercy. What else happened at the cross?

Rest assured, we didn't catch the Almighty off guard.

God told the prophet, Jeremiah, that before he ever formed him in his mother's womb, he gave him an appointment.

Us too! God had a good and perfect will for each of us before we were ever born. What is your purpose? What is his plan for you?

You may not have it titled or thought much about it, but you know at least a little. You can probably think of times when you were poked or prodded in a different direction. Maybe you remember a time being squeezed or molded into a different thought pattern. Or perhaps, you've had a barrier thrown up on one of life's paths while an entire wall collapsed on another.

That's divine direction and holy intervention. God's plan for you is in full motion, and it's invading every part of your life.

What if, at the cross, God had said, "Welcome to the family! I've got a purpose – a chore for you. Good luck with that."

Huh?

He didn't. No, what God did when he bathed you in mercy, was to immediately clothe you in grace.

You are now dressed in the best. Those ugly and tattered rags are gone! Marvelous grace adorns you.

Do you know what the most amazing, priceless thing about your new grace clothes is? They will always fit you. Grace will dress you for every occasion in your life. Every situation!

God told Paul, "My grace is all you need. My power works best in weakness." Paul's weaknesses could have been physical ailments, or the authorities questioning his apostleship, or a combination of many things.

For you – whether your weakness is a limitation you've allowed yourself, or a constraint that someone else has placed on you, know that you are just like Paul. God has an endless supply of grace. Where you are weak, he is all powerful.

Friend, at the cross, God gave you mercy, purpose, and grace to fulfill that purpose.

He is the King. You are his child. He's given you a task specifically designed for you; that only your shoes are meant to fill.

If you haven't experienced the mercy of God, this book will encourage and guide you to a better understanding of God's desire for you.

To my siblings-in-Christ, I hope you will consider what your purpose in God's plan is. Most important, I pray you will daily recognize God's grace and its potential through you.

God gave me mercy, purpose, and grace. Admittedly, I'm a work in progress. I'm Melissa Kirk, a *grace warrior*. My task is to encourage you to rise with me as a warrior for the Kingdom, bathed in mercy, clothed in grace.

# MERCY

*Definition: not getting what you deserve*

"Sweet mercy is nobility's true badge."

William Shakespeare

# Day 1 - MERCY

# In Worship

**Proclamation**

**Mercy**

Mercy is a gift from God, *the Father*, made possible through Jesus, *God's Son*. I accept the gift through faith in the victory over death by Jesus, *my Deliverer*.

**Why do I need mercy?**

God, who is just, cannot delight in the unrestored. I am unable to make myself worthy in the presence of the Almighty.

**Who grants mercy?**

God. Read *Ephesians 2:4-5.*

**Why does God grant mercy?**

He loves us. Read *John 3:16.*

**Receiving God's Word**

"The LORD passed in front of Moses, calling out, 'Yahweh! The LORD! The God of compassion and mercy! I am slow to anger and filled with unfailing love and faithfulness. I lavish unfailing love to a thousand generations. I forgive iniquity, rebellion, and sin. But I do not excuse the guilty. I lay the sins of the parents upon their children and grandchildren; the entire family is affected—even children in the third and fourth generations.'"

*Exodus 34:6-7*

**Connecting with God's Word**

How does God describe his mercy?

**Responding to God's Word**

Do you have something you want to say to God about mercy?

**Mercy**

What truth about mercy can you relate to today?

# Day 2 - MERCY

## Filthy Rags

King Saul received a command from God to go to battle. He was ordered to completely destroy the opposing nation. Spare no person, animal, or thing.

God meant business. Defeating the enemy spelled peace for his people. Destroying the plunder ensured outside influences couldn't seduce the people away from him.

King Saul went to war and won. But instead of following God's instructions, he kept everyone and everything *he* judged valuable.

What he considered useful contradicted God's perfect plan. He deliberately disobeyed, and the Bible says God was sorry he ever made Saul king. Read *I Samuel 15:1-10.*

God didn't need Saul's wisdom. He didn't even need his deeds. He only wanted Saul to trust and obey him.

What we have to offer isn't good enough. God calls our righteous acts filthy rags.

Like Saul, God simply wants us to trust and obey him. It begins by getting rid of the filthy rags.

**Receiving God's Word**

"We are all infected and impure with sin. When we display our righteous deeds, they are nothing but filthy rags. Like autumn leaves, we wither and fall, and our sins sweep us away like the wind. Yet no one calls on your name or pleads with you for mercy. Therefore, you have turned away from us and turned us over to our sins."

*Isaiah 64:6-7*

**Connecting with God's Word**

Why does God turn away from us?

**Responding to God's Word**

Is there anything you want to say to God?

**Mercy**

What truth about mercy can you relate to today?

# Day 3 - MERCY

## A Bath

I'd just made the bed and was bent over, picking up dirty clothes when I heard the bed springs squeak. I looked up to see my two-year-old grandson, Bostyn, jumping as high as he could, trying to touch the ceiling fan.

Catching him midair, I put him on the floor, smoothed the bedspread, and regathered the clothes.

Two steps outside the bedroom, I discovered the toddler sitting on top of the kitchen bar, playing with an ink pen. He'd used the computer unit as a step stool to climb onto the desk and then onto the countertop.

I scolded him and put him down, before squatting to push the unit under the desk. Confident any further temptation was removed, I headed to the washer.

Passing the bathroom, I spotted Bostyn balancing over the sink, his feet bouncing behind him. The faucet was on, and he happily splashed water everywhere.

That time, he received a finger-shaking-stop-it-right-now reprimand. I planted his feet firmly on the ground and my hands on my hips.

He took off. Rounding the corner, he scaled the kitchen table leg. Little hands and knees pattered across lunch's leftover spaghetti plate to the opposite side of the table.

Remembering the water was still running in the bathroom, I ran to turn it off. In the few seconds I was out of the room, Bostyn had climbed down and was scooting the chair toward the stove, dragging a stream of spilled juice with him.

I swooped him up and carried him into the living room, where we sunk to the floor. His over-stimulated, tired body wiggled and kicked while I held on tight, and the tears flowed – mostly mine!

In just a few short minutes, the little boy had added ink-stained hands, soapy arms, and spaghetti painted knees to his already dirty feet.

All I could say was, "You need a bath."

Just the other day, I was with family at the local pizza place for a birthday party. A half wall divided the private room from the general eating area.

There sat Bostyn, now four years old, on the ledge. He leaned back and propped up his foot. The small tennis shoe bounced in time to the music playing. I heard him tell my daughter, Ericka, “It’s okay, Mommy.”

At some point, we’ve all been like Bostyn, searching out the latest promises for a good time, grasping onto anything we thought would give us relief or satisfaction. Each unsuccessful exploration resulting in more gunk on us; overwhelming evidence that we didn’t find what we needed. Sometimes, we spend years before realizing that the answers to contentment aren’t found in our efforts.

God says, “You need a bath.”

**Receiving God's Word**

"Have mercy on me, O God, because of your unfailing love. Because of your great compassion, blot out the stain of my sins. Wash me clean from my guilt. Purify me from my sin."

*Psalm 51:1-2*

**Connecting with God's Word**

Have you ever felt too dirty to come clean? When?

**Responding to God's Word**

Is there anything you want to say to God?

**Mercy**

What truth about mercy can you relate to today?

# Day 4 - MERCY

## The Cross

God's mercy required a cross.

**Receiving God's Word**

**Do you need God's mercy?** "For everyone has sinned; we all fall short of God's glorious standard."

*Romans 3: 23*

**Why do you need God's mercy?** "For the wages of sin is death, but the free gift of God is eternal life through Christ Jesus our Lord."

*Romans 6:23*

**How did God show mercy?** "But God showed his great love for us by sending Christ to die for us while we were still sinners."

*Romans 5:8*

**What is my part in God's mercy?** "If you openly declare that Jesus is Lord and believe in your heart that God raised him from the dead, you will be saved. For it is by believing in your heart that you are made right with God, and it is by openly declaring your faith that you are saved."

*Romans 10:9-10*

**Will God's mercy work for me?** "For everyone who calls on the name of the LORD will be saved."

*Romans 10:13*

**How can I know God's mercy worked for me?** "So now there is no condemnation for those who belong to Christ Jesus. And because you belong to him, the power of the life-giving Spirit has freed you from the power of sin that leads to death."

*Romans 8: 1-2*

### Connecting with God's Word

Have you accepted God's mercy?

### Responding to God's Word

Is there anything you want to say to God?

### Mercy

What truth about mercy can you relate to today?

# Day 5 - MERCY

## Squeaky Clean

Parents breathe a little easier when bath time arrives. It usually means meals and playtime are done. Scraped knees have been kissed and the day's trials worked through.

Little dirty bodies with sticky fingers and tic-tac-toe marked legs glide into the shallow bubble bath water, and the hair washing battle begins.

Post battle, the rubber toys line the edge of the tub to drip, and the drain plug is pulled. The day's dirt gurgles down the drain.

The squeaky clean child with shriveled tipped fingers stands, their little arms crossing the sparkling body, knees trembling from the chill.

The once frazzled parent drapes a hooded towel around their loved one and carries them into another room. There's tickling and giggling while the youngster is dried off and dressed in clean pajamas.

All is well – until the little exploring eyes notice the sucker stuck in the rug.

**Receiving God's Word**

"Nothing in all creation is hidden from God. Everything is naked and exposed before his eyes, and he is the one to whom we are accountable. So then, since we have a great High Priest who has entered heaven, Jesus the Son of God, let us hold firmly to what we believe."

*Hebrews 4:13-14*

**Connecting with God's Word**

What does God see?

**Responding to God's Word**

Is there anything you want to say to God?

**Mercy**

What truth about mercy can you relate to today?

# Day 6 - MERCY

## The Throne

**Mercy changes how God sees us.** Our slate with him is clean. Read *Psalm 103*.

**Mercy changes our dependency.** The Holy Spirit helps us understand more about God. Read *I Corinthians 2:9-13.*

**Mercy changes our favorite meeting room.** We can approach God's throne boldly. Read *Hebrews 4:16.*

~A Note about Mercy~

Ask and you will receive.

**Receiving God's Word**

"This High Priest of ours understands our weaknesses, for he faced all of the same testings we do, yet he did not sin. So let us come boldly to the throne of our gracious God. There we will receive his mercy, and we will find grace to help us when we need it most."

*Hebrew 4:15-16*

**Connecting with God's Word**

What does God say about a Christ-Follower and sin?

**Responding to God's Word**

Is there anything you want to say to God?

**Mercy**

What truth about mercy can you relate to today?

# Day 7 - MERCY

## A New Way

**Mercy changes how we interact with others.**

Jacob favored his son, Joseph. It made his brothers so jealous, they sold him into slavery. To make matters worse, he was accused of misdoing and thrown into prison.

But God was watching over him. Joseph was released and even given a powerful position. Imagine his surprise when, years later, his brothers stood in front of him.

Due to a famine, they had traveled to Egypt in search of food. The men didn't recognize their grown brother, but Joseph knew them, and after testing their real intentions, he revealed his identity.

When they begged for forgiveness, not only did Joseph offer mercy, he extended grace by insisting their entire family move to safety in Egypt. Read *Genesis 37-46*.

In adversity, Joseph grew to trust God. He understood that God's purpose and mercy were much bigger than his family rivalry and personal suffering.

Will you give others mercy like God gave you?

**Receiving God's Word**

"Get rid of all bitterness, rage, anger, harsh words, and slander, as well as all types of evil behavior. Instead, be kind to each other, tenderhearted, forgiving one another, just as God through Christ has forgiven you."

*Ephesians 4:31-32*

**Connecting with God's Word**

What does mercy replace?

**Responding to God's Word**

Is there anything you want to say to God?

**Mercy**

What truth about mercy can you relate to today?

*Dear Lord,*

*Thank you for mercy. I pray that I will always remember your love and generosity. Help me to show others mercy.*

*Amen*

# GOD'S PLAN

*Definition: to build a family*

"Destiny waits in the hand of God, shaping the still unshapen."

T. S. Eliot

# Day 1 - GOD'S PLAN

# In Worship

### Proclamation

### God's Plan

God's plan is eternal. There has never been nor will ever be an existence able to foil God's perfect will. I cannot comprehend its vastness. Jesus is *Lord.*

### Why is God's Plan necessary?

God's plan gives a reason for his creation. Without God, I would not exist or have a purpose.

### Am I a part of God's Plan?

Yes. Read *Proverbs 16:9.*

### Will I understand God's Plan?

Yes. Read *I Corinthians 13:9-12.*

**Receiving God's Word**

"My thoughts are nothing like your thoughts," says the Lord. "And my ways are far beyond anything you could imagine. For just as the heavens are higher than the earth, so my ways are higher than your ways and my thoughts higher than your thoughts."

*Isaiah 55:8-9*

**Connecting with God's Word**

What does God say about his thoughts?

**Responding to God's Word**

Is there anything you want to say to God about his plan?

**God's Plan**

What truth about God's plan can you relate to today?

# Day 2 - GOD'S PLAN

## The Calling

"Samuel."

The priest's assistant heard correctly. Someone was calling him. After hearing his name three times, Eli, the priest, instructed the young man to listen one more time.

"Samuel! Samuel!"

It was God.

Samuel made a life changing decision and answered the call. "Speak, your servant is listening."

Because he was willing, God used Samuel in his plan many times. During his life, he served as a priest, prophet, and judge. God's messages weren't always easy to repeat, but Samuel obeyed anyway. Read *Samuel 3*.

God has a good and perfect will for his children. His plan is customized for the individual, each assignment designed to further his purpose.

His ultimate plan is to grow his family who will in turn bring glory to him.

Are you willing to answer God's call?

**Receiving God's Word**

"Even before he made the world, God loved us and chose us in Christ to be holy and without fault in his eyes. God decided in advance to adopt us into his own family by bringing us to himself through Jesus Christ."

*Ephesians 1:4-5*

**Connecting with God's Word**

How long has God wanted a family?

**Responding to God's Word**

Is there anything you want to say to God?

**God's Plan**

What truth about God's plan can you relate to today?

# Day 3 - GOD'S PLAN

## Fellowship

The conference was what I wanted. The topics sounded informative, the lodging looked beautiful, and the hands-on video training was only slightly intimidating. I calculated ninety-six hours I could spend fine-tuning my speaking craft. I even planned out my free time. Between classes, I'd retreat to my room, practice my speech, and edit my novel.

So, I registered and attempted to book a flight. The plane schedules were awful! Flying would take almost twice as long than if I drove. It dampened my enthusiasm. I reluctantly decided to drive.

The drive wasn't what I expected at all. The long road trip turned out to be easy, even relaxing. I spent the alone time alternating between speech practice and listening to Contemporary Christian music.

While unloading my vehicle at the lodge, another conference attendee, named Jerri, struck up a conversation about the protein drinks in my back seat. She obviously had better success with disciplined behavioral eating than me. She encouraged me, and I looked forward to visiting with her more. Jerri was the first of thirty-two women I would interact with over the next several days.

The conference wasn't what I was expecting. Instead of concentrating on book lessons, the days were spent building relationships with like-minded women who understood how I felt and what I wanted to achieve. We shared meals, stories, and heart-aches. We worshiped, laughed, danced, and sang. We worked together, cried together, and listened together as each testified about the goodness of God during video presentations.

The drive home wasn't what I expected, either. Music now alternated with reflections about lessons I learned from the other women. Granted, the classroom instructions were in depth and informative, but fellowshipping with my precious new-found friends was inspiring.

God derailed my plans for those ninety-six hours. He planned for a group of strangers to gather and fellowship with him. His purpose was for relationships to be built and strengthened for his kingdom work. I'm so thankful God has plans much loftier than mine.

God wants his children to know each other and visit.

He wants them to mentor and motivate one another.

Most of all, God wishes to be glorified. The Almighty wants his children to lay aside their plans and worries, and to recall his mercy and grace.

God's plan is energizing, and I am refreshed when I lay aside my plans to line up with his will. He takes great delight in that.

**Receiving God's Word**

"Let the message about Christ, in all its richness, fill your lives. Teach and counsel each other with all the wisdom he gives. Sing psalms and hymns and spiritual songs to God with thankful hearts. And whatever you do or say, do it as a representative of the Lord Jesus, giving thanks through him to God the Father."

*Colossians 3:16-17*

**Connecting with God's Word**

How do we live in fellowship with God?

**Responding to God's Word**

Is there anything you want to say to God?

**God's Plan**

What truth about God's plan can you relate to today?

# Day 4 - GOD'S PLAN

## Good for You

God's plan is good.

**Receiving God's Word**

**What is God's plan for me?** "For I know the plans I have for you," says the Lord. "They are plans for good and not for disaster, to give you a future and a hope."

*Jeremiah 29:11*

**What does God's plan do for me?** "But to all who believed him and accepted him, he gave the right to become children of God. They are reborn—not with a physical birth resulting from human passion or plan, but a birth that comes from God."

*John 1:12-13*

**Does God's plan include me?** "The Lord isn't really being slow about his promise, as some people think. No, he is being patient for your sake. He does not want anyone to be destroyed, but wants everyone to repent."

*II Peter 3:9*

**What is my part in God's plan?** "Therefore, go and make disciples of all the nations, baptizing them in the name of the Father and the Son and the Holy Spirit."

*Matthew 28:19*

**Will God's plan work for me?** "And we know that God causes everything to work together for the good of those who love God and are called according to his purpose for them."

*Romans 8:28*

**How can I know God's plan for me won't fail?** "Who then will condemn us? No one—for Christ Jesus died for us and was raised to life for us, and he is sitting in the place of honor at God's right hand, pleading for us."

*Romans 8:34*

**Connecting with God's Word**

What part of God's plan is most important to you?

**Responding to God's Word**

Is there anything you want to say to God?

**God's Plan**

What truth about God's plan can you relate to today?

# Day 5 - GOD'S PLAN

## Trust

One of the hardest things to do is to plan for the future. Often, when we manage to bring a project together, something happens to change everything.

Sometimes, we experience a sickness that interrupts our plan.

At times, another party changes their goal; as when a company scales back, or worse, shuts their door.

There's also those times when we get close to a goal, only to discover it isn't what we thought it would be.

In all these situations, we want and need direction.

Rest assured, God's plan is still at work. We can't see the entire picture, so it's essential we strengthen our relationship with the Almighty. The closer our kinship with him, the easier it is to trust him with the details.

Building relationships takes time and commitment, but it's important. Knowing God's plan is perfect hopefully encourages you to exchange with him regularly through prayer, study, and reflection.

**Receiving God's Word**

"Your own ears will hear him. Right behind you a voice will say, 'This is the way you should go' whether to the right or to the left."

*Isaiah 30:21*

**Connecting with God's Word**

What does God say about decision making?

**Responding to God's Word**

Is there anything you want to say to God?

**God's Plan**

What truth about God's plan can you relate to today?

# Day 6 - GOD'S PLAN

## The Path

**God's plan is revealed as we need it.** God tells us his plan is like a lamp that lights our way. Read *Psalm 119:89-112.*

**God's plan takes care of our needs.** We don't have to worry because God takes care of everything. Read *Matthew 6:25-33.*

**God's plan changes how we live.** We understand God expects us to prepare for the future. Read *Proverbs 31:10-31.*

~A Note about God's Plan~

God's plan is perfect because He is.

**Receiving God's Word**

"Stay on the path that the Lord your God has commanded you to follow. Then you will live long and prosperous lives in the land you are about to enter and occupy."

*Deuteronomy 5:33*

**Connecting with God's Word**

What does God say about staying on his path?

**Responding to God's Word**

Is there anything you want to say to God?

**God's Plan**

What truth about God's plan can you relate to today?

# Day 7 - GOD'S PLAN

## Faith

**God always finishes.**

God had plans for Abraham. He told the seventy-five-year-old man to leave home and go places he'd never been. He didn't go into the intricate details, but he made promises.

God promised to show him the way. He promised to make him into a great nation. Abraham would be blessed, and he'd be a blessing to others. That was a big plan!

Even though he couldn't see the road ahead, Abraham moved forward in obedience. It wasn't easy. Once, God instructed him to sacrifice his son, Isaac. Not understanding why, Abraham started to comply. Because he trusted and obeyed, God stopped him, and through Isaac, the Jewish nation was born. Read *Genesis 12-25*.

Abraham couldn't see the end result, either. He only knew he was to step out of his comfort zone and walk by faith.

Is your faith strong enough to believe, that even though you can't see the big picture, God is doing a good work in and through you and can do the same with your loved ones?

**Receiving God's Word**

"And I am certain that God, who began the good work within you, will continue his work until it is finally finished on the day when Christ Jesus returns."

*Philippians 1:6*

**Connecting with God's Word**

What does the scripture say about God's plan for you?

**Responding to God's Word**

Is there anything you want to say to God?

**God's Plan**

What truth about God's plan can you relate to today?

*Dear Father,*

*Thank you for including me in your plan. I pray that I will trust you and be obedient. Please encourage me when my faith falters.*

*Amen*

# MY PURPOSE

*Definition: to glorify God*

"Doing the will of God leaves me no time for disputing about His plans."

George MacDonald

# Day 1 - MY PURPOSE

## In Worship

**Proclamation**

**My Purpose**

My purpose is to bring glory to God. He is worthy of all honor and praise. He requires me to walk humbly and do what is good. God is *Sovereign.*

**Why is my purpose important?**

By testifying to the mighty works of God, his glory is made known to the world. There is no other god who can compare.

**Who decides my purpose?**

The Lord. *Read Micah 6:8.*

**Will I fully understand my purpose?**

Possibly not. Read *Proverbs 20:24.*

**Receiving God's Word**

"And we know that God causes everything to work together for the good of those who love God and are called according to his purpose for them. For God knew his people in advance, and he chose them to become like his Son, so that his Son would be the firstborn among many brothers and sisters. And having chosen them, he called them to come to him. And having called them, he gave them right standing with himself. And having given them right standing, he gave them his glory."

*Romans 8:28-30*

**Connecting with God's Word**

What does God do for those who love him?

**Responding to God's Word**

Do you have something you want to say to God about your purpose?

**My Purpose**

What truth about purpose is important to you today?

# Day 2 - MY PURPOSE

## The Surrender

God sent his Son, Jesus, to the world in human flesh. On earth, he experienced life as we do. He felt pain, disappointment, and failure, dealt with drama and conflict. He understood the battle with demonic spiritual forces while surrendering to God's plan.

Being perfect, he also knew the price that had to be paid to cover the wrongs and rebellion of humanity – death.

Right before he was arrested and wrongly accused, the gravity of his work became evident. Jesus prayed so earnestly, sweat drops of blood fell. He asked that if God was willing, to please take away the suffering he was about to endure. Then, he set an example for us and immediately submitted to God's plan and not his own.

His purpose was to obey the Father and die in our place. He did, and then, victoriously rose from the grave, and hope for us was born. Read *Luke 22 - 24.*

Our purpose is to accept Jesus as our deliverer and surrender to the will of God. Will you follow his example?

**Receiving God's Word**

"Father, if you are willing, please take this cup of suffering away from me. Yet I want your will to be done, not mine." Then an angel from heaven appeared and strengthened him. He prayed more fervently, and he was in such agony of spirit that his sweat fell to the ground like great drops of blood."

*Luke 22:42-44*

**Connecting with God's Word**

Describe how Jesus prayed.

**Responding to God's Word**

Is there anything you want to say to God?

**My Purpose**

What truth about purpose is important to you today?

# Day 3 - MY PURPOSE

## Service

My husband, sister-in-law, and I were out of town for their father's funeral. The night before, we settled into a nearby hotel and did what all modern, technically limited adults do; we checked our Facebook.

Almost immediately, I noticed a post about an accident near our home. Our daughter lives next door, so I checked in with her.

She was in shock. Three teenage girls were involved in a one-vehicle accident about a half-mile away. In the confusion, neighborhood parents were calling to make sure their kids were safe. Meanwhile, medical helicopters were sitting down, and the parents of the ones in the accident were being located.

The girls were friends of my grandchildren. One was my oldest grandson, Blake's, girlfriend.

Just a few weeks before, he had sat at my kitchen table and talked about beautiful Summer and the fact they had dated for a year. He cared a lot for her, and at Christmas, gave her a promise ring.

The accident happened during the holidays. Sadly, a short time after the horrible event, Summer's life on this earth ended. It devastated Blake, my other grandchildren, and our small community.

God used Blake during and after the tragedy. He used his youthful personality, his emotions, and his leadership to help the other teens in our town.

At the candlelight service, I watched as he walked around the room, consoling the other kids. He purposely sat next to the young girl who had been driving the vehicle, as if protecting her. He inquired about the third girl, who was hospitalized due to her injuries.

At Summer's funeral, he greeted the mourners, and during the service, he spoke wise words. He knelt by her elderly grandfather and patted the weeping man's hand.

Blake's purpose in the midst of the suffering was to comfort others. Even though he grieved too, he accepted his role and rose to the occasion.

God's healing presence was evident to others because Blake fulfilled his purpose. During the hardship, his service was needed and appreciated.

Serving God by showing his compassion through us is

our purpose. It brings God glory.

I pray my family will understand how God wants to use them during both the easy and difficult times in life. I pray I will fulfill the purposes God has for me. I pray the same for you.

**Receiving God's Word**

"For I was hungry, and you fed me. I was thirsty, and you gave me a drink. I was a stranger, and you invited me into your home. I was naked, and you gave me clothing. I was sick, and you cared for me. I was in prison, and you visited me." Then these righteous ones will reply, "Lord, when did we ever see you hungry and feed you? Or thirsty and give you something to drink? Or a stranger and show you hospitality? Or naked and give you clothing? When did we ever see you sick or in prison and visit you?" And the King will say, "I tell you the truth, when you did it to one of the least of these my brothers and sisters, you were doing it to me!"

*Matthew 25:35-40*

**Connecting with God's Word**

What does God say happens when we help others?

**Responding to God's Word**

Is there anything you want to say to God?

**My Purpose**

What truth about purpose is important to you today?

# Day 4 - MY PURPOSE

# The Assignment

My purpose is to do what God assigns.

**Receiving God's Word**

**What is my purpose?** "For God is working in you, giving you the desire and the power to do what pleases him."

*Philippians 2:13*

**How important is my purpose?** "For we are God's masterpiece. He has created us anew in Christ Jesus, so we can do the good things he planned for us long ago."

*Ephesians 2:10*

**Who does my purpose help**? "But you will receive power when the Holy Spirit comes upon you. And you will be my witnesses, telling people about me everywhere—in Jerusalem, throughout Judea, in Samaria, and to the ends of the earth."

*Acts 1:8*

**Does God help me fulfill my purpose?** "I cry out to God Most High, to God who will fulfill his purpose for me."

*Psalm 57:2*

**Will my purpose help me?** "And we know that God causes everything to work together for the good of those who love

God and are called according to his purpose for them."

*Romans 8:28*

**Can I fail my purpose?** "For I recognize my rebellion; it haunts me day and night. Against you, and you alone, have I sinned; I have done what is evil in your sight. You will be proved right in what you say, and your judgement against me is just."

*Psalm 51:3-4*

**Connecting with God's Word**

Who do we hurt when we rebel?

**Responding to God's Word**

Is there anything you want to say to God?

**My Purpose**

What truth about purpose is important to you today?

# Day 5 - MY PURPOSE

## Our Position

Our will that decides we recognize Jesus as Lord of our life is the same will that regularly blunders. Don't misunderstand. God's work in us doesn't fail. Christ-Followers are forever bathed in mercy. However, when we do not glorify God, we step out of his plan and our purpose stalls. God knows we are vulnerable children living in an imperfect world. That doesn't excuse our actions, just explains it.

We don't have to be bathed again. God's mercy continues to clean us. It's like God occasionally pulls out wet-wipes to remove the smudges.

That's what the apostle John explained to the Christians in his day. They would sin, but God was faithful to forgive their sins when they confessed.

It's the same for us. God expects us to regularly confess our sins. Routinely checking our attitudes and actions with Scripture catches errors early when they are easiest to line back up with God's plan. Doing so keeps us in the proper position to fulfill our purpose.

**Receiving God's Word**

"If we claim we have no sin, we are only fooling ourselves and not living in the truth. But if we confess our sins to him, he is faithful and just to forgive us our sins and to cleanse us from all wickedness."

*I John 1:8-9*

**Connecting with God's Word**

Does it worry or bother you to displease God? Why?

**Responding to God's Word**

Is there anything you want to say to God?

**My Purpose**

What truth about purpose is important to you today?

# Day 6 - MY PURPOSE

## The Focus

**God is pleased when I fulfill my purpose.** God rewards those who do his good works. Read *Ephesians 6:8.*

**My purpose changes my thoughts.** We concentrate on God's instructions. Read *Psalm 119:65-72.*

**My purpose changes my work habits.** We work to please God. Read *Colossians 3:23*

~A Note about My Purpose~

God disciplines and rewards his children.

**Receiving God's Word**

"So be careful how you live. Don't live like fools, but like those who are wise. Make the most of every opportunity in these evil days. Don't act thoughtlessly, but understand what the Lord wants you to do."

*Ephesians 5:15-17*

**Connecting with God's Word**

How does God want us to live?

**Responding to God's Word**

Is there anything you want to say to God?

**My Purpose**

What truth about purpose is important to you today?

# Day 7 - MY PURPOSE

## The Discipleship

**Our Purpose affects those around us.**

Eunice and Lois were Jewish women who converted to Christianity during the early days of the church. They understood their purpose and allowed God to use them.

Eunice had a son named Timothy. She and his grandmother, Lois, shared their faith with the youth, and he became a Christian too. They all became close friends with Paul during his ministry.

At a young age, Timothy became Paul's assistant and eventually represented his mentor during missionary trips.

Through the discipleship of Eunice, Lois, and Paul, Timothy was encouraged to work hard and grow in his faith. The elder man told him not to be concerned about being young or about *any* conflict associated with his position.

Timothy grew up during difficult times for the church, but because of the training and support he received from other Christians, he understood his purpose and allowed God to use him. Read *II Timothy 1:1-13.* Are you mentoring anyone?

### Receiving God's Word

"Jesus came and told his disciples, 'I have been given all authority in heaven and on earth. Therefore, go and make disciples of all the nations, baptizing them in the name of the Father and the Son and the Holy Spirit. Teach these new disciples to obey all the commands I have given you. And be sure of this: I am with you always, even to the end of the age.'"

*Matthew 28:18-20*

### Connecting with God's Word

What does God want us to do?

### Responding to God's Word

Is there anything you want to say to God?

### My Purpose

What truth about purpose is important to you today?

*Dear Lord,*

*Thank you for giving me purpose. I humbly surrender to your will. Open my mind and heart to opportunities of service. Help me tell others about your saving mercy and grace.*

*Amen*

# GRACE

*Definition: receiving what you don't deserve*

"Grace is but glory begun, and glory is but grace perfected."

Jonathan Edwards

# Day 1 - GRACE

## Worship

**Proclamation**

**Grace**

Grace is a gift from God, *the Father*, made possible through Jesus, *God's Son*. I accept the gift trough faith in the victory over death by Jesus, *my Messiah*.

**Why do I need grace?**

Only by God's grace is my faith found acceptable. My works are unable to save me. I am sorely weak and needy. In my weakness, the power of Jesus Christ is strengthened and found perfect.

**Who grants grace?**

God. Read *James 4:6.*

**Why does God grant grace?**

My works are not good enough. Read *Ephesians 2:8-9.*

**Receiving God's Word**

"God saved you by his grace when you believed. And you can't take credit for this; it is a gift from God. Salvation is not a reward for the good things we have done, so none of us can boast about it."

*Ephesians 2:8-9*

**Connecting with God's Word**

Can we do anything to earn salvation?

**Responding to God's Word**

Do you have something you want to say to God about grace?

**Grace**

What truth about grace can you relate to today?

# Day 2 - GRACE

## The Power

Paul was persecuting Christians, and God wanted him to stop. When light flooded from heaven and blinded the Jew, he obeyed, and his sight was restored.

The converted Pharisee immediately went to work fulfilling his purpose. Paul stopped murdering Christians and began to proclaim God's grace all across the Roman Empire.

Paul led an adventurous life as a missionary. He understood the need to fulfill his duty at any cost and tried to live in a way that would encourage others to have a relationship with God.

The missionary understood God's power. He begged God to take away a weakness that he called a thorn. But the Almighty refused, saying that his grace was all that was needed. Apostle Paul realized that God's power was better served in his weakness, so he boasted about his shortcoming instead. Read *Acts 9-11.*

Grace covers and protects God's child. Where we are weak, God's grace is all-powerful.

**Receiving God's Word**

"Three different times I begged the Lord to take it away. Each time he said, 'My grace is all you need. My power works best in weakness.' So now I am glad to boast about my weaknesses, so that the power of Christ can work through me. That's why I take pleasure in my weaknesses, and in the insults, hardships, persecutions, and troubles that I suffer for Christ. For when I am weak, then I am strong."

*II Corinthians 12:8-10*

**Connecting with God's Word**

Do you feel like you need a covering of grace? Have you felt the power of grace in your life?

**Responding to God's Word**

Is there anything you want to say to God?

**Grace**

What truth about grace can you relate to today?

# Day 3 - GRACE

# In Weakness

Many years ago, my husband, Larry, and I bought the old family home from his sister. There was just one condition. His elderly grandmother came with the house. It was fine with us.

Mrs. Jennie Bennett, in her eighties at the time, had a sweet temperament and was surprisingly able to maintain it when two adults, three teenagers, and a kitten seized the house.

She was gracious when I took over the kitchen. She was even more gracious complimenting the meals I prepared. I couldn't cook macaroni and cheese like she did, or so my husband said.

Once in a while, Mrs. Bennett propped up her feet in the living room chair, but most of the time, she sat at the kitchen table, content to play solitaire and watch soap operas on the little television in the corner.

If she had any concerns, she never voiced them to me. Her favorite saying was, "Anyway, anyhow."

Larry and I took a weekend trip one time and left her in charge of the teens. When we returned and asked if they behaved well, her favorite saying was a little more elaborate. "Anyway, anyhow, we made it." She was kind not to bother us with any details or tattle on the children.

As she grew old and frailer, she graciously accepted help. Larry watched over and cared for his grandmother's every need. If she required help with paperwork, adjusting the lamp, or walking to her bedroom, Larry was by her side.

When her health necessitated hospitalization, he spent many hours by her bed. When she passed from this life, he meticulously followed her instructions to the smallest notations scribbled on little slips of paper.

I didn't know Larry when he was young, but from the stories I've heard, his dear grandmother extended grace to the rambunctious boy many times. As he grew, I'm confident she extended as much grace needed to help Larry get through the life choices he made.

Watching Larry extend grace back to his grandmother was beautiful to me.

When Larry was young and weak, his grandmother's grace filled in the gaps as needed. In return, when Jennie Bennett grew old and frail, Larry's grace filled in the gaps for her.

It reminds me of the grace God offers all his children and how much he continues to extend it daily, enabling us to fulfill the purposes he assigns.

Marvelous grace. It fits every situation of our life.

**Receiving God's Word**

"And God will generously provide all you need. Then you will always have everything you need and plenty left over to share with others."

*II Corinthians 9:8*

**Connecting with God's Word**

Do you worry that your needs won't be taken care of?

**Responding to God's Word**

Is there anything you want to say to God?

**Grace**

What truth about grace can you relate to today?

# Day 4 - GRACE

## Grace Clothes

God's grace clothes us.

**Receiving God's Word**

**Do you need God's grace?** "For everyone has sinned; we all fall short of God's glorious standard."

*Romans 3:23*

**Why do you need God's grace?** "For the grace of God has been revealed, bringing salvation to all people."

*Titus 2:11*

**How did God show grace?** "So the Word became human and made his home among us. He was full of unfailing love and faithfulness, and we have seen his glory, the glory of the Father's one and only Son."

*John 1:14*

**What is my part in God's grace?** "Do not let any part of your body become an instrument of evil to serve sin. Instead, give yourselves completely to God, for you were dead, but now you have new life. So use your whole body as an instrument to do what is right for the glory of God. Sin is no longer your master, for you no longer live under the requirements of the law.

Instead, you live under the freedom of God's grace."

*Romans 6:13-14*

**Will God's grace work for me?** "For everyone who calls on the name of the LORD will be saved."

*Romans 10:13*

**How can I know God's grace worked for me?** "Yet God freely and graciously declares that we are righteous. He did this through Christ Jesus when he freed us from the penalty for our sins."

*Romans 3:24*

**Connecting with God's Word**

What does God's grace offer you?

**Responding to God's Word**

Is there anything you want to say to God?

**Grace**

What truth about grace can you relate to today?

# Day 5 - GRACE

# Kingdom Work

New Christ-Followers readily accept God's mercy. They sense a big plan in the works and want to be involved. The concept of grace is harder to process, but it is a pivotal element in the life of the Christian. Without understanding grace, Christians feel defeated when they commit a wrong. They lose sight that God takes care of the details, even through their shortcomings. Life without grace isn't God's plan.

God gives grace because we're vulnerable to Satan's attacks. The enemy takes great interest in preventing us from giving God glory. He paints false concepts of what our daily walk should look like and whispers condemnation when we fail.

Acknowledging God has the power to ward off the adversary is empowering. When we allow him to take charge, we soon shout in victory as he defeats the enemy's attack.

Grace is like new garments, clothing us in protection while God demolishes Satan's oppression. It reminds us our new birth is a gift from God, not from our accomplishments.

**Receiving God's Word**

"But my life is worth nothing to me unless I use it for finishing the work assigned me by the Lord Jesus—the work of telling others the Good News about the wonderful grace of God."

*Acts 20:24*

**Connecting with God's Word**

What is every Christ-Follower's purpose?

**Responding to God's Word**

Is there anything you want to say to God?

**Grace**

What truth about grace can you relate to today?

# Day 6 - GRACE

## The Blessing

**Grace changes how God sees us.** God heaps blessings on us. Read *John 1:15.*

**Grace changes our direction.** We turn from living unpleasing lives and devote ourselves to God. Read *Titus 2:12-13.*

**Grace changes how we see others.** We want others to receive the grace of God. Read *Hebrews 12:15.*

~A Note about Grace~

Grace is from God – to us – for others.

**Receiving God's Word**

"But whatever I am now, it is all because God poured out his special favor on me—and not without results."

*I Corinthians 15:10a*

**Connecting with God's Word**

Does God's grace work?

**Responding to God's Word**

Is there anything you want to say to God?

**Grace**

What truth about grace can you relate to today?

# Day 7 - GRACE

# Going the Distance

**Grace changes our endurance.**

The Bible calls Stephen a man full of God's grace and power. It was evident in the man's life, and his angry opposition falsely imprisoned him.

In today's world, many would consider that defeat, but God was at work. Stephen's *purpose* literally shone as his face became bright like an angel. With his adversaries' full attention, the glowing man gave a history lesson. His speech carried the listener through the Old Testament to their present time, proclaiming Jesus as the promised Messiah.

The people were enraged further, but Stephen didn't falter. He looked to heaven and declared that the Son of Man was standing at the right hand of the Father. The proclamation earned his martyrdom for God. The last words he spoke asked for forgiveness for his accusers. Stephen lived life like Jesus; proclaiming and forgiving. Read *Acts 6-7.*

Are you willing to go the distance for God no matter the outcome?

**Receiving God's Word**

"Stephen, a man full of God's grace and power, performed amazing miracles and signs among the people."

*Acts 6:8*

**Connecting with God's Word**

Have you ever endured persecution for God?

**Responding to God's Word**

Is there anything you want to say to God?

**Grace**

What truth about grace can you relate to today?

*Dear Lord,*

*Thank you for grace. Please use me so that your love and desires become evident to others. I gladly accept my weaknesses as opportunities for your power to shine.*

*Amen*

# Go in Grace

## *Mercy. God's Plan. My Purpose. Grace*

A lot happened at the cross. Not wanting you to get what you deserved, God stripped off your dirty life clothes and bathed you in mercy.

He took great delight in his brand-new child. His plan with you bloomed, giving you purpose to flourish and shine. To ensure you could, the Almighty dressed you in marvelous grace.

God said, "My grace is all you need. My power works best in weakness." *(II Corinthians 12:9)*

You can approach life as a Christ-Follower with confidence. While the world says you must fight to survive, God says to call on his grace.

Rise warrior. Go in grace.

"May God give you more and more grace and peace as you grow in your knowledge of God and Jesus our Lord. By his divine power, God has given us everything we need for living a godly life. We have received all of this by coming to know him, the one who called us to himself by means of his marvelous glory and excellence."

*II Peter 1:2-3*

If you haven't experienced God's mercy and grace, I pray you will have a conversation with him today. He wants you to be his child.

# READ MORE

# GROUP DISCUSSION NOTES

For success, be sure to plan ahead. Invite participants to the study. Conduct the meetings when it is most convenient for the group. Give attendees the book and assign the introduction and the first topic, "Mercy," to be completed before the first meeting. Set up everything for each meeting before the starting time. Review the week's discussion and when possible, enlist volunteers in advance for scripture readings. Keep the meeting short – an hour and one-half or less is plenty. Most important, keep it simple.

In advance: Prepare a poster board or dry erase board that has Hebrews 4:16 written on it. Use any Bible translation of the verse that works for your group. The following is from the New Living Translation:

"So let us come boldly to the throne of our gracious God. There we will receive his mercy, and we will find grace to help us when we need it most." *Hebrews 4:16*

Prepare a display that includes a cross and the poster board. It should be within easy reach of the leader.

# Optional

## activities to include in your meetings

› Refreshments. Decide if you will serve refreshments at the beginning or after the group discussion. Keep it consistent if possible.

› Have participants bring an item for the local food bank, nursing home, or children's home, etc. each week and assign someone to deliver the contributions after the final meeting.

› Ask volunteers in advance to do an activity. Examples are:

· Sing a hymn or lead the group in a song that fits the theme.

· Read a poem that fits the weekly theme.

· Watch a short YouTube video about the week's topic.

· Give a personal testimony.

· Lead a craft time that takes no more than fifteen minutes.

NOTE: Volunteers should have everything ready before the meeting begins so there won't be non-constructive down time.

ALSO: Door prizes are always fun.

# WEEK ONE – BATHED IN MERCY

Welcome everyone and allow time for introductions if necessary.

1. Point to the display and say, "For the next four weeks, we will work to memorize *Hebrews 4:16.* It is important to remember that we can approach God anytime and anywhere about anything. Each week, we will recite the verse, and then remove one-quarter of the scripture. By the end of our last meeting, we will be able to recite it from memory.

   As a group, read *Hebrews 4:16* from the poster board.

   Open in prayer.

2. Mercy – In Worship

   Responsive Reading: As a group, read aloud the first page of "In Worship" for the week of *Mercy*. The leader reads the words in bold letters followed by the group responding with the text. Enlist two participants to be prepared to read the included scriptures.

3. Any prearranged volunteer music, reading, or video would be appropriate now. However, any craft activity time would be better after group discussion.

4. Mercy – Filthy Rags

   Say "King Saul received a command from God. What was it and how did he respond?" Allow for discussion. Say "Have you ever taken matters into your own hands and not do what you knew God was asking you to do? How did it turn out?" Allow for discussion.

5. Mercy – A Bath

   Say "Have you ever felt too dirty to come clean? How did it feel once you were clean?" Allow for discussion.

6. Mercy – The Cross

   Ask for a volunteer to read *Romans 8:1-2.*

   Say "Our definition of mercy is 'not getting what you

deserve.' We have all sinned, but Jesus took our penalty. If we call on Jesus to save us, what are we free from?" Allow for discussion.

7. Mercy – Squeaky Clean

   Say "After becoming a Christ-Follower, we soon discover we still do and say wrong things. What should we do when we disappoint God?" Allow for discussion.

8. Mercy – The Throne

   Say "After we accept God's mercy, we have full access to him. He sends the Holy Spirit to help us. What does the Holy Spirit do?" Allow for discussion.

9. Mercy – A New Way

   Ask for a volunteer to read *Ephesians 4:31-32.*

   Say "Once we receive God's mercy, what are we to get rid of? How are we to treat others?" Allow for discussion.

   Say "Your assignment this week is to show mercy to others and study the topic of "God's Plan."

10. Prearranged volunteer crafts are appropriate here.

# WEEK TWO – GOD'S PLAN

Welcome everyone and allow time for introductions if necessary.

1. Point to the display and say, "I want to remind you that we are memorizing *Hebrews 4:16*. It is important to remember that we can approach God anytime and anywhere about anything.
   As a group, read Hebrews 4:16 from the board. Erase or mark out seven or eight words and repeat saying it. Open in prayer.
2. God's Plan – In Worship

Responsive Reading: As a group, read aloud the first page of "In Worship" for the week of *God's Plan*. The leader reads the words in bold letters followed by the group responding with the text. Enlist two participants to be prepared to read the included scriptures.

3. Any prearranged volunteer music, reading, or video would be appropriate now. However, any craft activity time would be better after group discussion.

4. God's Plan – The Calling
   Say "Samuel heard God call him. Have you ever felt a special calling from God? What was it or what did it feel like?" Allow for discussion.

5. God's Plan – Fellowship
   Say "How important is fellowship with God and other Christ-Followers? What is the experience like?" Allow for discussion.

6. God's Plan – Good for You
   Ask for a volunteer to read *Jeremiah 29:11.*
   Say "What are some of God's good plans for his children?" Allow for discussion.

7. God's Plan – Trust

Say "What is the hardest thing for you to trust God with?" Allow for discussion.

8. God's Plan – The Path

   Say "What is our responsibility in God's plan? What is God's?" Allow for discussion.

9. God's Plan – Faith

   Ask for a volunteer to read *Philippians 1:6*.

   Say "What do you think made Abraham's obedience difficult? How difficult is it to have faith in God?" Allow for discussion.

   Say "Your assignment this week is to consider God's plan with you and study the topic of "My Purpose."

10. Prearranged volunteer crafts are appropriate here.

# WEEK THREE – MY PURPOSE

Welcome everyone and allow time for introductions if necessary.

1. Point to the display and say, "I want to remind you that we are memorizing *Hebrews 4:16.* It is important to remember that we can approach God anytime and anywhere about anything.
   As a group, read Hebrews 4:16 from the board. Erase or mark out seven or eight words and repeat saying it. Open in prayer.

2. God's Plan – In Worship

Responsive Reading: As a group, read aloud the first page of "In Worship" for the week of *My Purpose*. The leader reads the words in bold letters followed by the group responding with the text. Enlist two participants to be prepared to read the included scriptures.

3. Any prearranged volunteer music, reading, or video would be appropriate now. However, any craft activity time would be better after group discussion.

4. God's Plan – The Surrender

   Say "Jesus fully surrendered to the will of God. Being perfect but in human form, he understood the difficulty of obeying. How difficult is it for you to surrender and obey?" Allow for discussion.

5. God's Plan – Service

   Say "Our purpose is always to bring glory to God. What are some ways we do that? Name some easy ways and some difficult ways." Allow for discussion.

6. God's Plan – The Assignment

   Ask for a volunteer to read *Philippians 2:13.*

   Say "What are some things we do that please God?" Allow for discussion.

7. God's Plan – Our Position

   Say "How does it feel to regularly battle a particular sin? What should you do?" Allow for discussion.

8. God's Plan – The Focus

   Say "What are some things we can do to successfully fulfill our purpose?" Allow for discussion.

9. God's Plan – The Discipleship

   Ask for a volunteer to read *Matthew 28:18-20.*

   Say "What does Jesus tell us to do? What does he promise?" Allow for discussion.

   Say "Your assignment this week is to consider God's purpose with you and study the topic of "Grace."

10. Prearranged volunteer crafts are appropriate here.

# WEEK FOUR – CLOTHED IN GRACE

Welcome everyone and allow time for introductions if necessary.

1. Point to the display and say, "We have been memorizing *Hebrews 4:16*. It is important to remember that we can approach God anytime and anywhere about anything."
   As a group, read Hebrews 4:16 from the board. Remove the board and repeat the verse. Congratulate the group for their hard work.

Open in prayer.

2. God's Plan – In Worship

   Responsive Reading: As a group, read aloud the first page of "In Worship" for the week of *Grace*. The leader reads the words in bold letters followed by the group responding with the text. Enlist two participants to be prepared to read the included scriptures.

3. Any prearranged volunteer music, reading, or video would be appropriate now. However, any craft activity time would be better after group discussion.

4. God's Plan – The Power

   Say "Paul begged God to remove a weakness and God refused. Have you ever felt as if God was refusing to remove one of your weaknesses so his power would be evident? Would you like to share the experience?" Allow for discussion.

5. God's Plan – In Weakness

   Say "How important is it to extend grace to others? How does it feel to receive help from others?" Allow for discussion.

6. God's Plan – Grace Clothes

   Ask for a volunteer to read *Titus 2:11.*

   Ask for a volunteer to read *Romans 6:13-14.*

Say "What does the revelation of God's grace do? How do living under the requirements of the law and living under the freedom of grace differ?" Allow for discussion.

7. God's Plan – Kingdom Work

   Say "What work did Jesus assign? How much importance do you place on the assignment?" Allow for discussion.

8. God's Plan – The Blessing

   Say "What are ways God has blessed you?" Allow for discussion.

9. God's Plan – Going the Distance

   Ask for a volunteer to read *Acts 6:8*.

   Say "Stephen was martyred for the cause of Christ. What do you think enabled him to face death and ask that the stone-throwers be forgiven? Could you face persecution?" Allow for discussion.

10. Prearranged volunteer crafts are appropriate here.

Excerpt

# GRACE WARRIOR

## *At the King's Command*

Grace Warrior Devotional Series

# The Edict

My mother loves the McIntosh variety apple. She says it's full of flavor, easy to digest, and bakes well. When they're in season, she loads up. I can be sure she will send some home with me because she knows I agree – they are delicious.

What makes it good is everything under its skin. The fruit thrives with a strong core, seed, flesh, and stem. Properly grown and harvested, it's pleasing to the taste buds. Just as God intended.

In similar fashion, everything good about us is under

our skin in impalpable life sources created by God; wholly designed to glorify him. As Christ-Followers, we are a sampling of his perfect flavor.

To enable us to yield the proper taste of his goodness, he issued an edict he calls the most important command.

"And you must love the Lord your God with all your heart, all your soul, all your mind, and all your strength."

*Mark 12:30*

This is a direct order between him and us which God doesn't trivialize. Our adoption into the kingdom came at the highest cost; the blood of Jesus. To say that he wants all our energy concentrated on all things godly would be wrong. He doesn't want it. He demands it.

The duty appears daunting, but here's the beautiful thing. He *created* our heart, soul, mind, and strength, and knows their full potential. If we yield to his authority, our human limitations cease to matter. God has high expectations and gives us his unlimited, all-powerful grace to overshadow our weaknesses.

We will never be able to fully embrace this command. The closest we come is if we willingly lay ourselves to be martyred. However, he knows we are imperfect people and is not only faithful to put our perceived failed attempts in right standing, but to also use them to bring attention to him.

What's under your skin? Does your heart beat for God? Does your soul reveal you prefer him over everything else? Is your mind calculating every move to benefit the Almighty? Are you using every ounce of your strength to follow his instruction?

It's our call to obedience. Friend, embrace it. God created you. He walks life's path with you. He preserves your life for the number of days he determines right. He's prepared an everlasting home for you. He loves you and has exciting plans for you. He watches over you as the apple of his eye.

Your next breath is dependent on him.

God adds a second command that he says is just as important.

"The second is equally important: 'Love your neighbor as yourself.' No other commandment is greater than these."

*Mark 12:31*

I believe obeying the second edict will subconsciously happen if we are complying with the first.

With this devotion, my prayer is that Christ-Followers will find the determination to follow God's command by reflecting on his Word.

If you aren't a Christ-Follower, I pray that you will come to an understanding of God's authority and your position with him.

Excerpt

# ADVENT

## *Celebrate the Coming*

Grace Warrior Devotional Series

# Advent

I love Christmas! But, in years past, the chaotic, commercialized, celebration of Christmas sucked the life out of me.

There's the *Final Sales Event of the Season* that happens every weekend. Charity drives, company socials, family dinners, parades, church plays, and band concerts fill the calendar. Apparently sleep isn't necessary the last six weeks of the year.

Christmas decorations crowding out pumpkins before

the first leaf falls bugs me. Happy Holidays versus Merry Christmas debates on social media are annoying. One Christmas carol per sixty Santa Baby songs on the radio bothers me. And, the Babe-in-a-manger piece haphazardly stuffed between a Ninja Turtle Cowabunga Christmas plaque and a snow globe with Frosty in beachwear sends me over the edge.

For years, I lit up the entire house with twinkling lights. Bah humbug putting that mess away. Once, I did the reverse and simplified. No one appreciated the oranges, apples, and walnuts in their stocking.

My strategies weren't working, but with three children, eleven grandchildren, and a great-grandchild, a full retreat wasn't an option. So, I had a conversation with God after the last yuletide, and through a summer of reflection, I realized the problem. I was misinterpreting the season's rules of engagement. Until now, my battle cry was:

*It's Christmas. I will survive.*

*I will decorate my home fashionably. It's Christmas.*

*I will prepare a large family meal. It's Christmas.*

*I will buy lots of presents. It's Christmas.*

*I will insist everyone experience peace and goodwill or else!*

*It's Christmas. I will survive.*

I had it wrong, and my life was void of all that the Advent season celebrated: hope, peace, joy, and love.

God reminded me that the world's idea of celebration contradicts his, but it's *his* battle, not mine.

He reiterated that Christmas doesn't stop people from hurting. It doesn't take away restlessness or discouragement or loneliness. Hope, peace, joy and love so desperately sought after is found in Christ alone; not in the celebration.

He requested I recall my rank. You may have noticed a whole lot of *I's* in the above thoughts. He did too. God wants my participation in his kingdom affairs, *under* his authority.

So, you'll still find me in the midst of the chaotic, commercialized, celebration of Christmas, but hopefully a new me; with a clearer understanding of God's seasonal rules of engagement. My duty as a grace warrior for the kingdom is to follow his simple directives: converse and share.

When my hands dig through the sixty percent off pile of pajamas, hope can be shared by buying a set for the children's shelter and praying for the child who wears them. While waiting in line behind the young couple who is trying to decide if they can afford the milk, diapers, *and* discounted plastic toy truck, peace can be shared by slipping a ten dollar bill their way and inviting them to the free church community meal. Joy can be shared by reciting a few lines from *The Magnificat* with a new mother. As the community parade floats pass by, love can be shared by telling the person standing next to me about God's faithfulness. Here's my new battle cry.

*God sent his Son, Jesus. He is coming again, soon.*

*God sent a star to light our way. Celebrate and share hope.*

*God's heavenly hosts cried out. Celebrate and share peace.*

*God's gift is eternal life. Celebrate and share joy.*

*God's gift is available to all. Celebrate and share love.*

*God sent his Son, Jesus. He is coming again, soon.*

Whether your Advent season is packed with festivities, or mostly alone time, God's directives are the same: converse and share.

The gifts people want are your time, your smile, your touch, and most importantly, your testimony of the celebration *you* have because you received God's gift of eternal life; free from death and decay.

If you haven't accepted his gift, my prayer is that you'll have a personal conversation with the Almighty. It's because of his Son; we celebrate the Advent season.

# Thank you

Thank you to my fellow Christian Communicators: Shelli Wenschlag, Elaine Q. Potts, Michelle Viscuse, Tope Keku, Lyneta Smith, and Sheryl Buckner. Your testimonials are very dear to me. They communicate your personalities beautifully.

Thank you to the rest of my family and friends for your encouraging words.

And an extra special *thank you* to my husband, Larry, who spent many hours with the television volume turned very low so I could concentrate on my writing.

Thank you to my readers. I wish you the best God has to offer in all seasons of your life.

To follow my Grace Warrior blog, kindly visit www.MelissaKirk.ORG and subscribe to receive e-mail notifications. I promise not to flood your inboxes.

# Special Links

**Grace Warrior Blog**

www.MelissaKirk.ORG or www.TheGraceWarrior.com

**Facebook - Personal**

Melissa C Kirk

**Facebook – Author**

MelissaKirkAuthor

**Pinterest**

MelissaCKirk

**Twitter**

@melissackirk

**Google +**

Melissa C Kirk Grace Warrior

**Instagram**

Melissackirk

GRACE WARRIOR – *At the King's Command*

ADVENT – *Celebrate the Coming*

www.MelissaKirk.ORG or www.Amazon.com

Go in God's Grace

Made in the USA
Columbia, SC
16 March 2021

33946290R00086